Shop-fl
Christi

H. Frank Dee

Inter-Varsity Press

Inter-Varsity Fellowship
39 Bedford Square
London WC1B 3EY

First edition July 1972

ISBN 0 85110 452 5

Printed in Great Britain by
Richard Clay (The Chaucer Press), Ltd.,
Bungay, Suffolk

Illustrations by Norman Stone

A lot of profound books have been written about work; this isn't in that tradition. It's the simple thoughts of a simple workman. My hope is that they will help those who have recently entered industry or intend doing so when they finish their student days, or those doing a polytechnic sandwhich course. (Other readers are welcome at no extra charge.) If this book helps you to see that industry is as much part of God's world as a field of corn or a cathedral spire, that shovelling coal or building bicycles can be as honouring to God as preaching in a pulpit or teaching in a school, I will be happy.

My grateful thanks to Miss Sarah Greenaway and Mrs Jean Booth who deciphered and typed my scrawl again and again. My thanks also to my wife and friends who constantly encouraged me to start, continue and finish this book.

H.F.D.

Contents

1 Why work anyway?

A pal of mine used to say, 'Why should the working man work when he's got the health and strength to lie in bed?'

Why do we work? Is it just to earn money to live? Or is there more to it than that?

Perhaps you know the tale about the elderly Negro Christian in Chicago who was asked what his work was. He replied: 'I pack meat to live; but my work is preaching the gospel.'

I thought it was a wonderful tale at one time. But is this really the Christian attitude? Was it the attitude of Christ? It would mean that, though Jesus fashioned wood for a living for the greater part of His life, He worked only for the last three years.

In any case it doesn't fit our experience. We all know the satisfaction of slogging away hard all day and finishing tired but triumphant. Many people go on working when they could well afford to stop. Why?

God and the working man

Jesus gave a clue to the answer when He said, 'My Father is working still and I am working.' Even God works!

We see it right at the beginning of Genesis:

In the beginning God created the heavens and the earth.

God not only worked but also found satisfaction in His work:

God saw everything that he had made, and behold, it was very good.

Well, you may say, that's God, not man. But we are made in the image of God. God said:

Let us make man in our image.

God didn't put Adam and Eve in the garden of Eden to lie under a tree and occasionally reach up for a hand of bananas or a juicy pineapple:

The Lord God took the man and put him in the garden of Eden to till it and keep it.

This was work! Man was working, even before he sinned, while he was still perfect and walking and talking with God.

Jesus the carpenter was doing His Father's work as much as Jesus the preacher. When Jesus was baptized by John, God said, 'This is my beloved Son, with whom I am well pleased.' This was *before* Jesus started His ministry. The perfect life included the perfect carpentry.

We work because God intended us to work. This is how we were made.

Lord of the earth

But there is another reason why we should work: because God, when He made man, gave him a job, to subdue the earth and to have dominion over every living thing. The garden of Eden not only contained vegetation but mineral wealth. We are partners with God in work.

When Sir Edmund Hillary and Sherpa Tensing reached the top of Mount Everest they were subduing the earth.

So was Sir Alexander Fleming when he discovered penicillin (he was also having dominion over living things – germs). We are subduing the earth when we contribute to the world of work, whether as coal-miner or chemist, dustman or director.

Modern industry is one of the means God uses to enable us to do this. The raw materials of nature are turned into products for the benefit of man and society, for instance to feed the hungry and heal the sick through farm machinery and fertilizers, drugs and surgical and medical instruments. Printing presses and electrical firms provide the communications vital for man to talk to man. And by modern industry we mean the men who work in industry. We are helping to fulfil God's command.

Jesus taught us to pray, 'Give us this day our daily bread'. Work is the way by which God has ordained that we obtain it.

When things go wrong

However much we believe this, however much we enjoy our work, however keen we are, sometimes things go wrong. We find it becomes boring, frustrating, back-breaking and plain hard. We do not find it as God said, that it is 'very good'. Why? Sin! It spoils everything, including work. God said to Adam after he had sinned:

Because you have listened to the voice of your wife,
and have eaten of the tree
of which I commanded you,
'You shall not eat of it,'
cursed is the ground because of you;
in toil you shall eat of it all the days of your life;
thorns and thistles it shall bring forth to you;
and you shall eat the plants of the field.
In the sweat of your face
you shall eat bread

till you return to the ground,
for out of it you were taken;
you are dust,
and to dust you shall return.

I believe God in His mercy uses even the sweat and toil for our good.

The old saying that Satan finds work for idle hands to do is very true. There is probably more sin in the idle gossip at a cocktail party than on an assembly line at Fords. Not because Ford workers are better – but because they are busier.

This is borne out by Paul's words to the Thessalonians:

If anyone will not work, let him not eat. For we hear that some of you are living in idleness, mere busybodies, not doing any work.

It is important to notice Paul says 'will not work', not 'cannot work'. It is a stricture against the idle, not the infirm, aged or unemployed.

We also have our industrial equivalents to thorns and thistles because man has chosen to go his way; he knows best. Man wanted to be free from God and has become a slave to sin. The results are seen in all sorts of ways: the-least-work-for-the-most-money attitude of some employees; the-least-wages-and-most-production attitude of some employers. It is seen in badly designed equipment, in bad workmanship and in skimped materials. It is seen in industrial strife and unemployment; in industrial diseases and accidents, in excessive profits and excessive wages.

As Christians we believe God when He says, 'Sin shall not have dominion over you', and we must live out our Christianity in our work. 'We are a new creation', Paul said, and our work should reflect this.

Archbishop William Temple said, 'We should regard our work as worship . . . breath, brains and brawn all for God.'

Do you think Jesus in the carpenter's shop for fifteen to eighteen years fretted and fumed and longed to be finished so He could get off to preach, or do you think He laboured turning out the best, the finest oxen yokes, ploughs, benches and house beams ever seen in Nazareth?

Purpose of work

We work because God intended us to from the beginning: not only to make money, or even that we might be able to feed and clothe ourselves, but for the good of others, for the good of society in which God has placed us.

This is the difference which being a Christian makes.

> *Let the thief no longer steal, but rather let him labour doing honest work with his hands, so that he may be able to give to them in need.*

Do you get that? Not only to provide for ourselves and for our own family; we will be able to give to those in need.

Those in need may be next door – or in Peru. Our giving may be through a relief fund or a works collection. But work is the way you get the money to give.

So to work is to fulfil God's original purpose for us in creation. We are helping to control and use the world's resources, however small our own job may be, if we are helping to make something of use to our fellow-men.

And to work is to fulfil God's purpose for us as Christians in His new creation. We help to carry out Jesus' command: that we should love our neighbour as ourselves.

What work?

We have seen that man was made to work, but what work? It's fairly easy to decide what not to do. Anything that does not glorify God or isn't loving my neighbour. So for me working in the gambling industry or brewing and its retail

ENGINEERS WANTED
JOIN THE PROFESSIONALS
OR ELSE!
JOIN INDUSTRY
WHERE THERES MUCK THERES MONEY!!
BE A PART-TIME BRAIN-SURGEON
A-LEVELS? O-LEVELS? C.S.E? 11-PLUS? DOG LICENCE? PARKING TICKET? DOCTORS NOTE
WE HAVE A PLACE FOR YOU
WHY NOT BE AN OPTICIAN
JOIN THE NAVY AND SEE THE SEA
SKOOL LEEVERS
HEY LOWER PONGINGTONS LOCAL AND INDUSTRIAL SEWER WORKS ARE LOOKING FOR YOU
CAREERS

What work?

outlets are 'out'. You will, no doubt, have your own list of things that are definitely 'out'. But what is 'in'?

Sometimes I think we take the 'he who has clean hands' too literally. God gives different people different gifts.

One of my favourite portions of Scripture is:

> *The Lord said to Moses, 'See I have called by name Bezalel . . . and I have filled him with the Spirit of God, with ability and intelligence, with knowledge and all craftsmanship, to devise artistic designs, to work in gold, silver, and bronze, in cutting stones for setting and in carving wood . . . and I have given to all able men ability.'*

Imagine his father saying, 'But Bezalel is going into the office with me. I don't want him getting his hands hard or dirty cutting stones', or his mother saying, 'What will the neighbours think if he comes home in his overalls?'

Filled with the Spirit of God to work, to do manual work for the glory of God. Our world tends to exalt the clean-hand, white-collar jobs and, regretfully, the church has tended to do the same.

In saying that manual work isn't to be despised, the contrary must not be assumed. Abraham and Joseph knew what manual work was all about but they were clearly highly skilled administrators. The same could be said of Moses, scholar, soldier, statesman, but he learned his obedience in forty years of manual work. God gives gifts to men, manual, administrative and technical. The clean hands and the dirty to do His will.

The important thing is to choose carefully what your future work will be, praying about it, consulting your parents and considering what abilities God has given you.

Better to be a good dustman than a bad Prime Minister.

Bible passages to look up

About work

Genesis 1:1, 26; 2:2, 15
Proverbs 6:6–11; 16:26
John 5:17
1 Thessalonians 4:11–12

Work spoiled

Genesis 3:17–19
Isaiah 44:10–20

Working for others

Acts 20:34–35
Ephesians 4:28
2 Thessalonians 3:7–11

Some workers in the Bible

Genesis 4:20–21
Exodus 1:8–14; 31:1–11
1 Kings 6
Nehemiah 2:17; 4:6; 6:1–4
Jeremiah 18:1–6
Luke 2:8; 5:3–7
Acts 10:6; 18:1–3

2 Get stuck in!

I thought my first foreman was the most foul-mouthed, obscene man who ever existed. An ex-naval stoker who seemed to have been involved in plenty of the world's worst ports, he delighted in regaling all and sundry with his experiences.

The impact upon me was immediate and devastating. I wanted to crawl away and hide. This experience was made worse when a man known to be a church-goer joined the firm soon afterwards and I found he joined in with the best of them – or rather the worst of them. Most young Christians seem to have faced this in some form or other, and react in various ways.

Wanting to crawl away and hide is a natural feeling. But it can so easily lead to shutting yourself up within yourself, a sort of mental monastery.

Seeing no evil, hearing no evil, speaking no evil, can easily degenerate into seeing no good, hearing no good, speaking no good.

At a conference some time ago the secretary of a National Christian organization said, 'Industry is rotten from top to bottom. We are only in it to evangelize.' I sympathize with his outburst. I understand his feelings. But what he said is plainly unbiblical.

Jesus said, 'You are the salt of the earth.' If you just keep salt in the salt-cellar it won't be much use. It needs sprinkling. Salt stops the good going bad. It flavours the insipid. It cleanses and stops the rot. I believe this is part of the Christian vocation in industry. Too many of us are more like the other members of the condiment family, peppery or vinegary!

Just how to go about being salt is the difficulty; how to be in the world but not of the world. Jesus clearly recognized this when He prayed, 'I am not praying that you will take them out of the world but that you will keep them from the evil one.' Read His whole prayer for yourself in John 17.

Jesus involved Himself deeply in the life of His time, in the carpenter's shop, at weddings, funerals and feasts. Whether cooking a breakfast or cleansing the temple, He is never the innocent bystander.

Things didn't just happen to Jesus. He made them happen. Or, as Lord Baden-Powell, the founder of the Boy Scouts, put it, it is a question of actively doing good, not passively being good.

So as Christians we must be those who set the standards – make the pace.

Making the pace

'Don't try to keep up with the Joneses – it is covetous' is often the message from our pulpits. My message is different: '*Be a Jones*'.

Have you noticed that if one chap paints his house others follow because it makes their paint look shabby? If Joe cuts his lawn Bill's wife will notice how long their grass is. There has to be a first painter, a first lawn-trimmer.

As Christians we should be the pace-makers: making the pace in the punctuality stakes but not making the pace as the first blokes to knock off work. But we shouldn't keep at it simply to impress the boss.

My first foreman

Making the pace in good conscientious work, but helping the chap who finds the going hard – we don't want to shine so that others are made to look dull.

Up with the front runners in saying 'thank you' to the floor sweeper as well as the foreman; always ready to say sorry when we are wrong; courteous to all. Paul said,

Show yourself in all respects a model of good deeds.

Be up the front when a newcomer is experiencing those first few hours of bewilderment. He will need a friend when he doesn't know the routine or where the toilets, stores or anything else are. It is peculiar how few firms take the trouble to make new employees welcome by showing them around. The first things he needs to know are those mentioned and what your name is, when tea-break is (has he got a cup?), what the food is like in the canteen or the local café, and a reassuring word: 'Don't worry, you will be able to cope.' Invitations to the Christian Fellowship can wait until later.

Make the pace with the conversations you hold, with 'sound words that cannot be criticized', to quote Paul again. It's useless getting hot under the collar about other people's filthy suggestions if your remarks about a girl walking through the workshop sparked them off. Watch your lips.

From the same mouth come blessing and cursing. My brethren, this ought not to be so.

So says James, the patron saint of the workshop.

'Quit your holy huddle'

After the failure of a series of evangelistic concerts put on by Musical Gospel Outreach, John Webb, the producer, asked, 'Where are the non-Christians?' and answered himself, '*Obviously not where the Christians are!*'

He continued, 'Of course it's more comfortable to be

with Christians. Then you face no awkward problems . . . but had Jesus taken that attitude He'd probably have stayed in the carpenter's shop and never made Calvary.' I disagree in part: the Son would never have left heaven; the carpenter's shop had problems as well.

The failure of those concerts was not that they didn't have a good show, or a good audience, but the wrong audience. They were all Christians and it was aimed at a fifty-fifty crowd – half non-Christians.

'You are the salt of the earth', said Jesus. Instead we are being pickled in our brine tubs, we who follow the One who said, 'Be of good cheer. I have overcome the world.' We are still in the upper room for fear of the Jews – and anybody else who says 'boo' to us.

Is it more comfortable? About as comfortable as an armchair in a stuffy room on a warm summer's day. So let's get out and enjoy the sunshine even if we do have to face the occasional wasp.

Join the firm's fire brigade, train as a first-aider, be a contributing member of the community. Play with the firm's football team if that's your game, or cricket, rugby, table tennis, etc. Join the photographic society, music club or horticultural section. Go to the speedway, football or other entertainment with the fellows you work with.

Don't always sit with Christian friends in the canteen (assuming there are others), but with the crowd you work with or play games with.

Where Christian principles are concerned, decide where you stand and why. Stick to it and do not waver. Your friends may well drop you and they may very well not.

Coping with the problems

There are problems. There were when Jesus went to that Pharisee's house on the sabbath to a feast and they 'planted' a man with the dropsy in front of Him, but He didn't duck the issue. He never refused the invitation. He invited Himself to Zacchaeus's house. He talked to a woman – a Samaritan woman – which was contrary to custom.

You too will face problems if you get involved. For instance, you might win the firm's table tennis trophy and it is presented at the annual dinner and dance. The horticultural society might have its annual show on Saturday, but the clearing up done on Sunday.

If you go to a dinner and dance – you can eat! If you feel dancing is 'out' for you (it's 'out' for me for no other reason than that I was born with two left legs!), well, you can talk and be sociable. If alcoholic drink is something you would rather not take, and I'm in that class, today the field is wide open from Coke to coffee, so why be embarrassed?

Clearing up after a show or a fête is something that calls for tact and, boy, can we lack that! Let it be known early if you feel unable to do it Sunday and volunteer to do the preliminary clearing on Saturday evening.

A greater problem for me is Christmas eve, or the day before the Christmas holiday. I think it neither sensible nor festive to switch off machines and wander around saying 'Merry Christmas' and drinking until the firm lets you go home.

One year I was working on the axle assembly line of a car plant at Christmas time. A few days previous to the holiday the chargehand said to me quite casually, 'You don't drink, do you, Frank?' I agreed I didn't. Presently he transferred me to working the hoist lifting the axles off the line. I either stacked them or put them straight onto the main assembly line. I was quite pleased; it was a good little number and the hoist did all the heavy work.

During the next few days we over-produced to the extent that all the available floor space was stacked with spare axles. On Christmas eve after lunch the line stopped and the chargehand and the rest of the gang retreated to a quiet corner for a 'booze-up', leaving me to feed the main assembly line with the stacked axles. I was not over-pleased, but I really had nothing to complain about. I was doing what I was paid for, the time passed quickly and my head was clearer than theirs the next morning. It was the Lord's overruling.

What I usually do is work while it is possible, then have a good clear up; you accumulate a lot of 'toot' and rubbish in twelve months. I polish up my tools, return all the 'Merry Christmases' aimed in my direction, and try to refrain from being 'holier than thou' in my attitude. If you can influence others to refrain from this annual ritual it is certainly a good bit of salt-spreading.

The real and only safeguard is a close walk with the Lord.

If you find yourself swearing, if only under your breath, take it to the Lord in repentance. If the pin-up that disgraces the walls excites your imagination, take it to the Lord. If you are tempted to listen to the dirty jokes that fly around, the answer is the same. Cleansing begins and goes on at Calvary. If you walk away when dirty jokes are told, at first they may try to get you to listen, but normally they soon stop telling them when you are around.

You obviously can influence what is put up in the immediate area around your own machine or working space, and although some people will persist with nude and near-nude pin-ups, others will acknowledge that your standards are the right ones and remove them.

Prayer is your most powerful weapon here. It is still true that more things are wrought by prayer than men dream of.

James starts his letter:

> *Count it all joy, brothers, when you meet various trials*

and goes on to say,

If any of you lacks wisdom, let him ask God, who gives to all men generously.

In his last chapter he reminds us

The prayer of a righteous man has great power in its effects.

Bible passages to look up

The Christian in the world

Matthew 5:1–20
John 17:1–26
Philippians 2:1–16a

Some Christian standards

Ephesians 6:5–9
Colossians 3:22 – 4:1
Titus 2:7–13

Your talk

Proverbs 16:23–24; 25:11
Colossians 4:5–6
James 1:26; 3:2–12
1 Peter 3:9–12

Your walk

Matthew 5:43–48; 7:12
Romans 13:8–14
Galatians 6:2–10
Titus 3:2

3 Have a flutter!

Life is a gamble! . . . You surely don't object to raffles! How narrow can you get? It's for a good cause!

How do you deal with the constant stream of salesmen who work for the goddess of chance? Well, first, why do you object to gambling? What is wrong with a flutter?

It is necessary to be quite sure in your own mind that gambling in all its forms is wrong and to know why it is wrong.

I have no intention of dealing with this in detail. Let me give you just three pointers:

1. Having committed your life into God's hand, to give your money to Lady Luck is hardly faith.

2. It is Satan's voice that whispers 'it is for a good cause', while the actual motive is to gain a lot by chancing a little.

3. If I love my neighbour as myself I will not want to make him poorer by getting richer myself.

Saying 'no'

That said, you are still faced with the problem of how to say 'No'.

If it is a football pool agent or a profit-making gamble of any kind I find a courteous but firm 'No, thank you' is fairly easy, but when it's for a good cause, that's the rub; what then?

Personally, if it is something I feel is worth supporting I offer the price of a ticket or more, courteously explaining that I don't want to take part in the draw. Sometimes the money is accepted, sometimes it isn't. Sometimes the opportunity to say why you don't gamble is presented. If the retort is 'What a lot of old rubbish that is!' don't worry; that was how they treated your Lord.

A far more difficult thing is when the money goes to something where you share in the fruits of the gamble. National Premium Bond draws are in this category. They help to finance our country but we don't agree with them; it's one of the things we need to repent of for our nation.

Some firms' Sports Clubs run draws on all the big horse races. If you take part in the Sports Club activities you share the fruits of these gambles. Our Shop Stewards' Committee runs a regular draw for funds and I share the fruits.

How can you get over this one? Sometimes you can't; you have to accept that, just as part of our national economy is financed by a gamble, so are some of our more local activities.

If you play football, cricket, darts or take part in any club activity, you must recognize that part of the support comes from a source you are opposed to, and make your decision whether to continue or not in that knowledge. I can't (and would not) make up your mind for you. I can only tell you of my experience.

When I was first asked to be a shop steward I realized that one of the duties was to collect the dues for the Shop Stewards' Draw. I made it perfectly plain that I could not agree to this. Nevertheless I was elected and someone else collected the dues. Recognizing that this put an extra burden upon someone else I undertook all the workshop collections for retirements, deaths, sickness, etc. Later I

RAFFLE GOOD CAUSE
CHEA
SPEND
SWEEP STAKE
SPECIAL OFFER
RAFFLE
WORKS POOLS SYNDICATE
RAFFLE EVEN BETTER CAUSE

saw that for the efficient running of the committee and for certain hardship cases some funds were necessary and I shared the spoils of gambling in that any out-of-pocket expenses were covered from that source.

There never was, and never will be, a gamble in which losing investors will not eventually cry 'fiddle, swindle', etc. This happened in our case and during a debate on the situation I pressed the point of direct giving and got the reply 'It will never work'.

It transpired that two-thirds of the proceeds of this draw went in prizes and one-third went to the fund. So I went to people who were not in the Shop Stewards' Draw and asked them to contribute directly to the fund (at that time it was fourpence a week). In quite a short time – under a fortnight – I had a third of the workshop personnel contributing by this means.

Shop-floor trading

One thing that has crept into industry in the last few years is the shop-floor trader. The chap who can offer you anything from razor blades to shirts, cheap!

I have been told that a stall was set up in a ladies' loo in one factory. Certainly all sorts of merchandise is offered for sale, and when Christmas approaches some factories begin to resemble Eastern bazaars. Well, it's cheaper than the shops, it's handy and it's all honestly come by. Why not buy?

When a chap comes up to you and says, 'Want a watch cheap, smuggled of course?' (apart from the fact that it's probably only a cheap non-smuggled watch being sold dear to mugs) your course is clear: it's dishonest, don't touch it! But with honestly come-by stuff, what's the harm? Ask yourself these questions:

Is the trader being paid by the firm while he conducts his own business?

Is he avoiding having to pay rates and rents like a normal shopkeeper by taking advantage of his employer's premises?

Has purchase tax been paid on the goods?

Last, but not least, is it really cheap, or just shoddy?

My answer would be, 'If in doubt, don't' (and I don't).

A job on the side

What about 'foreigners' or 'homers'? The name varies, but it means doing a job for yourself on the firm's premises, often in the firm's time, and with the firm's material.

The easy, simple answer is 'Don't'. Things aren't always simple and easy, though.

Your motor-bike conked out on the way to work. It only needs a nipple soldered onto the clutch cable and it will save pushing the bike home, half an hour's hard slog.

A plastic knob on mum's cooker has split. It can be araldited together in two minutes and tons of the stuff goes to waste all the time.

They want two quid for a spare part for my fishing-line and I can knock it up on my lathe in ten minutes.

What's the harm?

It does rather depend on factory rules. Some managements allow operators to use machines in lunch-hours, some don't. If they don't, there is probably a good reason why, such as insurance, or because the privilege has been abused in the past. Some firms will allow you to do a 'get-you-home job'; some won't.

What is important is that your Christian witness should not be spoiled. What Christian principles are involved?

Honesty. If you can't be open and honest in doing it, either it's wrong or you ought to get a ruling from the management on what's allowed and what isn't. Christians must be seen to be honest before all men.

Stealing from your firm or from anyone else, either materials or time, is a basic offence against society, and forbidden in the Ten Commandments. If you want to use the firm's materials, ask whether you can pay for them, or if they are waste get a clear ruling about it.

Waste? Nature is very bountiful. The oak-tree produces hundreds of acorns to reproduce itself each year. In its life-time it must produce hundreds of thousands. But the surplus isn't wasted, as squirrels and other animals could testify. Our Lord fed 5,000 men, apart from women and children, but instructed the disciples to collect up the remains. And they did – twelve baskets full!

Industry is often much less careful to see that there is no waste. Although many companies have salvage and reclamation programmes or departments, others do not. Some of the best companies allow employees to buy damaged or surplus goods, and others have staff trading schemes which allow employees to buy their produce at cost or near cost price.

Naturally there are always some who will abuse such schemes. A firm discovered that the odd ends of packing-case wood being taken home for firewood were, in fact, their planks being put through the circular saw just to provide kindling for employees' fires. In another firm record players were being deliberately damaged slightly when an employee had a customer for one.

What of the odd nuts and bolts, short lengths of cable, scraps of sheet metal, or rod, etc?

In my particular factory we use a lot of plastic tubing, and I wondered why the odd six-inch lengths were in such great demand – until I found they were ideal for petrol feed-pipes on auto-cycles.

All this stuff is going to waste, into the rubbish bin or incinerator – the firm doesn't want it, it's scrap, you can't return it to the stores. Why not take it and use it? It saves waste!

Discussing this with a Christian friend at work, I asked him, 'What about the Old Testament scripture which says

"You shall not muzzle an ox when it treads out the grain"?' In other words you should let the ox pick up what it can while it's on the job! Didn't Paul say that this was written for the sake of men? Does that mean we ought to be allowed to take what we need from our work?

Charlie, a shrewd old tool-maker, replied, 'That's fair enough for girls in a sweet factory. But what about those who work at the Bank of England printing works?'

This I feel gives the right answer for a Christian. **Waste is indeed wicked, but so is stealing.** Paul was talking about people's right to be paid for a job of work. If you can use waste products with the company's permission, do so. If the firm on the other hand has a policy that allows good stuff to be wasted but not taken by employees, that is their decision, wrong though it may be. Taking without the owner's consent is plain stealing, and 'You shall not steal' is still a valid commandment.

Perhaps some day you will be in a position to influence your company's policy on salvage and waste. It's worth finding out more about *God's* attitude to these things.

Bible passages to look up

Gambling

Proverbs 16:8
Jeremiah 17:9–11
Romans 13:8–10

Giving an answer

Proverbs 15:1
Colossians 4:6
Titus 3:2

Honesty

Exodus 20:15
Deuteronomy 23:24–25
Luke 16:10–12
Titus 2:10
1 Peter 4:14

Sharing work's reward

Ezekiel 34:17–22
1 Corinthians 9:8–12
Ephesians 4:28

4 Give us this day

Work is the means God has provided for us to get the bread He gives. Not only that, but to return to Him part of our earnings and to help others less fortunate than ourselves.

In the old Testament tithing (giving a tenth of the produce to the Lord) was one method of returning to God His own wealth. Leaving the corners of the fields uncut and not stripping the vines completely provided for the less fortunate.

The thrill of the first pay-packet is a never-to-be-repeated joy. One of my children declares the first thing she is going to do when she goes to work is to buy her mother a dishwasher. Not entirely a noble thought (she hates washing up the crocks) but partly so.

'When I get money of my own'; the sense of independence and the sense of contributing to the family purse – perhaps a sense of greed . . . *but it's not our own.*

Giving to others

Over the Stock Exchange in London are the words 'The earth is the Lord's and the fullness thereof'. The founders of that institution recognized the basic fact that they handled what was, in fact, the property of their Creator to whom they were responsible.

All that we have is Thine alone,
A trust, O Lord, from Thee.

The first call on our money is God. His work at home and abroad. So start right by considering prayerfully how much you should give back to God. Many Christians take the Old Testament tithe or tenth as their standard. Paul says, 'Each one must do as he has made up his mind, not reluctantly or under compulsion, for God loves a cheerful giver.'

In the passage (opposite the front door) of our council house my mother had a picture of a lovely 'olde worlde' thatched cottage with roses round the door and underneath the words 'Home, the place where you get treated best and grumble most.'

We never let her get away with that. Reversing the three-ply board we stuck on the back a picture of a ramshackle hut cut out of a missionary magazine and with the aid of a red-hot poker, wrote 'Home, the place your money gets taken every Friday.'

'Cusses!' my mother would say good-naturedly, turning it to the right side. It was five to one in our favour so usually 'the money gets taken side' was on display. It was literally true: we took our pay-packets home and they were taken and we were given our pocket money back. Gradually we were given control of more and more as we grew older. First, pocket money; later we bought some of our own clothes; then all our clothes; and finally we had the pay-packet and gave Mum our 'keep'.

I've always been grateful for the discipline of money which my parents taught me, although it was partly an enforced discipline caused by unemployment and near poverty.

Whether you hand over the packet or hand over your 'keep', you have the privilege of helping support the family home. Often parents feel they ought not to take anything because your pay is small, but it is right that they should. It is the only way to learn the value of money and the control of it.

We were discussing the parable of Lazarus and the rich man. How the poor beggar was obviously a man of faith but had none of this world's goods. Charlie suddenly said, 'But we are the rich of this world!' The statement shattered us. Mentally we had all aligned ourselves with the poor beggar – faithful, but hard up!

Charlie was right: we do feast sumptuously, we are clothed in fine linen – when we compare ourselves with the plight of the beggar of Calcutta, the Indians in the Argentine Chaco or the Christians in Eastern Europe.

You will recall the condemnation of the rich man in the Bible story: you in your life-time received the good things.

In the first chapter of this book I quoted Paul as saying that 'we earn so we can help those in need' and in his letter to Corinth he tells the Christians to put aside their money as God has prospered them for the needy.

Personally, I find a regular amount through Oxfam Pledge Giving Scheme the best way for me. Take your choice. Tear Fund, War on Want, Inter Church Aid and the hundreds of home societies such as Shelter, Dr Barnardo's, Help the Aged, etc.

It's also a good plan to keep a little aside for the needy you will meet in your own locality.

The following extract is from a letter in our church magazine, 'Christmas can be a lonely time for those who, like me, live alone. You can imagine my delight on receiving a Christmas card from "one of the youngsters of St Mary's". Inside was a 50p piece – a very thoughtful and useful gift.'

'*It is more blessed to give than to receive.*' This could well be paraphrased '*It's more fun*'.

Spending money

I know when I started work my pay-packet very rarely lasted till the next pay-day. An evening paper and a bag of peanuts each day coming home from work, subs for Scouts and I was broke.

It's not difficult to spend money, but it's wise to save. For your holidays, for the future, as yet unseen need. It's wise to put aside money for clothing. If you haven't already got one start an account at a bank or the post office.

We live in an age which is marvellous in many ways, but one of the less attractive features is the appeal to greed, selfishness and covetousness in advertising.

It's your money they are after or, to be more precise, the money God has entrusted to you as His steward. That word conjures up a man who looks after you on a boat. The word servant is hardly better because it seems to be associated with housework and butlers and maids. Perhaps investment manager would be better, although it sounds over-important. The point is, so many things which advertisers tell you are essential to modern living are often just unnecessary extravagance that you will soon regret. Think hard before you part with your brass.

Mr Micawber's other piece of advice is still valid, even though his currency is outdated. 'Annual income twenty pounds, annual expenditure nineteen nineteen six, result happiness. Annual income twenty pounds, annual expenditure twenty pounds ought and six, result misery!'

Getting rich

The natural reaction to outgoings being greater than income is to increase your income, and as a trade unionist I agree with Paul that 'The labourer is worthy of his hire.'

How far should we take this search for riches? I believe it was Lord Nuffield who, when asked how much money is enough, said 'Just a pound more than you have got.'

I prefer the answer of another rich man:

Do not toil to acquire wealth:
be wise enough to desist.
When your eye lights upon it, it is gone;
for suddenly it takes itself wings.

The man who wrote that was the richest man on earth but when God had said to him years before, 'What shall I give you?' he chose an 'understanding mind' and God added riches. Neither was he afraid of hard work. He also wrote 'Whatever your hand finds to do, do it with your might.'

Solomon studied this business of wealth in great depth and had a lot to say about it. It is worth your while looking it up (see the book of Proverbs). Certainly there are rich men in the Bible who found favour with God: Abraham – the friend of God, Job – my servant Job, David – a man after God's own heart, Solomon, etc., but they seem to be tribal or national leaders. The main theme seems to be a warning against the snares of riches. From Solomon ('Better a poor man who walks in his integrity than a rich man who is perverse in his ways') to the merchants of Revelation, weeping and mourning for Babylon because nobody buys their cargo of gold, silver, jewels and all the other luxuries any more.

A modern fallacy has arisen that if you are not doing all right financially, then something is spiritually wrong. Examine the facts.

If that were true, Lazarus would have gone to hell and the rich man to heaven.

If it were true, our brethren in India, Africa and South America must be an extremely godless lot and we in affluent Britain must be basking in God's sunshine.

Returning missionaries (they must be backsliders because they are so badly paid) tell a story of radiant overseas Christians and shudder at our pagan society.

Paul, that spiritual giant whom none of us would dare

measure ourselves against, was penniless at the height of his spiritual power. '*For his sake I suffered the loss of all things and counted them as refuse.*'

Taking part in a Counsellor's Training Course in preparation for an evangelistic crusade the leader was talking of Abraham being extremely wealthy. 'There's nothing wrong with being rich,' he said. 'You all want to be rich, don't you?' 'Yes,' the large assembly yelled back, and then laughed rather self-consciously. Personally I just felt rather sick that this was a gathering of people who follow the One who said, 'But woe to you that are rich, for you have received your consolation.'

Not that money itself is evil, or wealth of any description, but man with his natural bias for the bad easily misuses it and loves it. Jesus put His finger on it by saying, 'It will be hard for a rich man to enter the kingdom of heaven.'

I remember the Rev. Eddie Stride startling us all when he said from his pulpit, '*You can't take it with you but you can send it ahead.*' He filled in the details by pointing out that Jesus told us to lay up treasure in heaven where it won't rust or rot or go mouldy and there are no rogues to rob us.

So if you ever get rich, remember your responsibility to others and your danger if you aren't careful and prayerful!

Bible passages to look up

Wealth belongs to God

Genesis 13:15–18	Job 1:1–10
Deuteronomy 8:6–18; 11:14–16	Psalms 50:10–12; 89:11
1 Chronicles 29:11–14	Haggai 2:8

Giving to God

Exodus 35:4–9, 20–29; 36:6–7	Malachi 3:6–10
1 Chronicles 29:1–9	Matthew 23:23–24
2 Chronicles 31:4–10	Mark 12:41–44

Giving to others

Leviticus 19:9–10
Deuteronomy 15:7–11
1 Chronicles 16:1–3
Isaiah 58:6–7
James 2:14–17

The peril of riches

Deuteronomy 8:10–18
Psalms 62:8–12
Proverbs 23:4–5; 28:6–7, 20–22
Ecclesiastes 5:10–17
Matthew 6:19–24
Luke 12:16–20; 18:18–30
1 Timothy 6:5–19
James 5:1–6

5 'I am black but comely'

'Why is that wog over there on the staff and he's only been in the firm five minutes?'

The inquiry came from an irate craftsman who pointed in the direction of the electronics test bay. 'Do you mean that new test engineer?' I ask. 'It's company policy for test and inspection to be on the staff.'

Whether it is right that some employees should clock on and others sign on, some be paid for sickness, others not, was not the point at issue. What was at issue was the colour of a man's skin. Not the ability of an intelligent, highly skilled Sikh to do a good job, but a highly emotive response to fear.

It's not always like that. 'I bet none of you can get a tan like this in a fortnight's holiday.' The speaker was a young Jamaican grinning all over his handsome bronze face. He addressed the workshop in general, confident of the acceptance of his joke, secure in the knowledge that he was among friends.

In the last few years the increase of overseas workers has made a new situation in industry. Men with pink colour skin fearing men with brown colour skin and vice versa for a lot of different reasons.

It is not by any means all one-sided. While I was serving

in the Air Force at one point a few of us were posted to a bomb dump in Cambridgeshire. We found the amazing situation of a large group of West Indians insisting on sitting at different tables in the dining hall and yet accusing their English comrades of operating a colour bar. Being new to the camp we queued for our food and sat down at the nearest vacant table which happened to be one occupied by several Jamaicans, who promptly got up and changed tables.

The contradictory stories about the start of the trouble made it impossible to know where the blame lay. Ironically we were supposed to be comrades fighting to free the world from Hitler, the champion of racial prejudice and hatred.

The problem isn't new but Christians have a special responsibility in this. We worship a God who '*made of one blood all nations to dwell on the face of the earth*'. His Son came to earth, an Asian, whose parents were forced to emigrate to North Africa. His cross was carried by a black man.

In another chapter I quoted Moses forbidding oppression whether '*he is one of your brothers or a sojourner*'. Later God *through Moses* makes a statement that I believe to be one of the kingpins of our behaviour:

> *When a stranger sojourns with you in your land, you shall not do him wrong. The stranger who sojourns with you shall be to you as the native among you, and you shall love him as yourself.*

This makes the matter quite clear; people of other nationalities are not second-class citizens to do the rough, hard, low-paid, dirty work. They are 'to you as a native', a fellow-Cockney, Scouse, Geordie, Brummie or whatever part of this island you come from.

Moreover many of them are natives. Recently we have become aware of this as a coloured comedian with a broad Yorkshire accent has graced the little screen. My generation followed with keen interest the fortunes of Randolph

Turpin, while today his nephew, Jackie Turpin, boxes his way to fame. Like many more they are as British as the flag. Second, third and even fourth generation Englishmen.

Part of my boyhood I lived in a road near West India Docks close to the area called Chinatown. Our street was quite a 'United Nations' but I don't recall any of us being particularly worried about our different origins. We had grown up with them and they with us.

The crunch comes when a 'foreign' element 'invades' our home ground, whether that home ground is our factory, school or district. The newcomers may well cling together because they share common culture, language, religion, etc. The natives may feel threatened, their jobs, homes, customs at peril.

We need to understand the other fellow's point of view, try to put ourselves into his shoes. If we are white try to understand the black who has built a wall around himself after being constantly buffetted. If we are from a different ethnic group we need to understand the Anglo-Saxon who sees his district changing, his way of life apparently disappearing.

One of the girls who typed the manuscript of this book is black (and very comely). She works for the Housing Department of a local authority. One of her duties is to interview people regarding rent rebates. One morning she received a telephone call: 'A Mr Lillywhite to see you.' Going into the outer office she inquired of a man sitting there, 'Mr Lillywhite?' 'That's more than you can say', he replied aggressively. She told me the story between peals of laughter, which her mother joined with great gusto.

The man was waiting for an official interview – always a nerve-racking affair. He wanted his rent reduced, so he was on the receiving end and probably felt it was a bit humiliating (though it isn't) and then this official turned out to be a woman and black! She understood all that and instead of being angry in her turn, saw the humour of the situation and could laugh and put him at his ease.

Peter, in his first epistle, puts it this way:

> *Never pay back a bad turn with a bad turn or an insult with another insult, but on the contrary, pay back with good. For this is your calling – to do good and one day inherit all the goodness of God* (J. B. Phillips' translation).

The apostle Peter wasn't always free from fault on this issue. He had no bother in mixing with other groups when he was alone with them but when some Jews came on the scene he withdrew from eating with the Gentiles. Paul says, '*I opposed him to his face.*'

It is so easy not to do what we know is right because our own group will disapprove, and this is never more true than in the racial context.

God, through Moses, spoke very strongly on this issue:

> *Cursed be he who perverts the justice due to the sojourner.*

It naturally works both ways. God also said,

> *You shall have one law for the sojourner and for the native: for I am the Lord your God.*

In industry customs and practices have grown up which both management and workers know and conform to. It is important that people coming in from other cultural backgrounds try to understand and obey these rules.

It is so easy to be prejudiced and so difficult to be unbiased in these things. As Christians we are not called to be unbiased but to lean over backwards for the other chap.

One of Jesus' best-known parables is on this racial theme, namely the Good Samaritan.

Who was his neighbour?

The one who showed mercy!

Go and do likewise.

I recall reading a comment by a West Indian worker, 'Yes, they are friendly at work but they never invite you to their homes.'

I know a man who noticed the bike of a Pakistani he worked with was unsafe and commented on it. The man had been quite unable to find anybody willing to repair it or understand what he wanted. The following evening my friend took his workmate to a local cycle dealer with whom he had made arrangements to do the job. While the work was being carried out they went home for a meal together, at my pal's house. Because of his guest's concern that the meal contained no pork (it was a bangers and mash tea and the hostess had anticipated the problem) a lively conversation was soon going on about their respective religions and the opportunity arose to witness to the saving power of Christ.

That, of course, is our final ground, for in Christ there is neither Jew nor Greek; we are all one in Christ Jesus.

Bible passages to look up

Leviticus 19:33–34; 24:10–22
Jeremiah 7:5–7
Matthew 25:35
Luke 10:25–37
Acts 17:26
Galatians 2:11–14
Hebrews 13:2
1 Peter 3:9–15

6 'The best that I can be'

'To be the best, the best that I can be.'

What does that hymn mean for the ordinary chap or girl like you or me in factory or workshop, a mill or a mine, or for that matter any other place where ordinary people work?

Do we equate 'best' with 'highest'?

Does to be the best I can for God mean getting on and up?

Well, does it?

It most certainly means being honest in all our dealings.

When Paul wrote to Titus whom he had left behind in Crete, he had some harsh things to say about the Cretans. Among other things he reckoned them to be lazy, piggish and liars. Some had been converted, however, and so Titus is told to remind them 'to be ready for honest work'. Earlier in the letter slaves are told not to be light-fingered, to give satisfaction in every respect and, for me the most difficult bit of all, not to be sullen or perverse.

If I had been carted off my land, made to work for nothing, the sole property of my master to do as he pleased with, and then somebody had said 'Don't be sullen', I reckon I might have found it a bit hard to take. Paul didn't say that; he said,

So that you are a living testimony to Christ.

PROMOTIONS
THIS WEEK
TNT

Elsewhere he tells Christians, that is us, to act

> *not with eyeservice, as men-pleasers, but in singleness of heart, fearing the Lord.*

The very fact that we are being honest will not necessarily make us popular.

I can recall times when being honest has made me extremely unpopular. On the only occasion that I have got the sack it was for telling my employer that he was robbing his customers – and he was! So honesty won't necessarily guarantee promotion (although it may). Neither will hard work.

Is promotion always God's will for Christians?

Certainly the 'in-fighting' for promotion is out for us. We cannot and must not join the rat-race where no holds are barred and the devil takes the hindmost. In sober truth, Satan takes the lot in that situation.

David Orman, Secretary of the Liverpool Diocese Board of Finance, tells of when he was in industry and one of the bright young men in the office went out to the toilet. While he was out the phone rang and the Managing Director asked for him. One of the other man in the office answered the phone and said quite casually, 'I'm sorry, sir, we haven't seen him this morning.'

> *The rat-race is not for heirs (hares) of God.*

A young Christian said to me, 'I'll be glad to get out of the planning office. I have never worked in such a horrible atmosphere, all stabbing each other in the back . . . and it doesn't matter if you are a fellow-Christian.'

Christians getting bitter and twisted because they think they are entitled to the promotion somebody else got are hardly following Paul's example:

> *I have learned in whatever state I am to be content.*

We need the conviction of the fiery furnace trio as they faced a furious despot:

Our God whom we serve is able to deliver us . . .; and he will deliver us. . . . But if not, . . . we will not serve your gods.

God may call you to promotion but if He doesn't, do not worship the god of advancement. Getting on can be covetousness rather than being the best we can be for God.

'Consider your call, brothers.' God's best for you may well be the shop floor. He needs His people in every situation and could call you to forego promotion in His service.

We applaud the doctor who gives up a promising career in one of our major medical establishments to go with the Leprosy Mission to a remote hospital in a strange country, and we are right.

We admire the teacher who takes up an appointment in a Missionary Society, rather than one at a school in England, and we are right.

And you are right if God's place for you is to be a joiner in a shipyard in the north-east, or a process worker in a chemical plant in the Midlands. You are right to be there and you should be content. While we can hardly expect other people to admire or applaud, the church, i.e. your fellow-Christians, should recognize your calling.

The church is at its weakest at the work-bench level, in the downtown areas, and on council housing estates, because Christians have not had the vision to see that these are parts of *all the world that we are to go into to preach the gospel.*

David Sheppard has written:

There is a proper ambition, wanting the best for yourself and your family. But the command is, 'Love your neighbour as yourself'. This means that when decisions about moving house or taking a 'better' job come up, our neighbour's interest should go into the scale as well as those of ourselves and our family. To turn our back on worldliness means learning to sit loose to the god of status, security and money.

We have a perfect example in the Perfect Man.

Jesus rose from a carpenter's shop to a wooden cross. Therefore God has highly exalted Him and bestowed in Him a name above every name.

Bible passages to look up

Honest work

Titus 3:1 | 1 Peter 2:18–20

Contentment

Philippians 4:11–13 | 1 Timothy 6:6

God's place for us

Isaiah 6:8–13 | Luke 8:39; 18:28–30

7 Time off

God rested on the seventh day of creation. Jesus said to His close friends after a period of work, 'Come away by yourselves to a lonely place, and rest a while.' Mark comments, 'For many were coming and going, and they had no leisure even to eat.'

Starting work is a tiring business. At first you will probably find you are very tired by knocking-off time. So don't overfill your evenings with activities (even Christian activities). You need to rest a while.

God has a lot to say about this in the Bible, but it's funny how often men think they know better than God. Many modern-day illnesses can be traced back to not following the Maker's instruction manual. Mention Sunday overtime in any factory and there is no lack of volunteers. In fact, for all overtime it's usually easy to get people to work. Most people can use the extra cash.

There are other considerations which apply to all men (for God made all men) but which we, as Christians, should be especially keen to adhere to.

The Maker's rhythm is six, one, six, one, and if we ignore this divine timing the human mechanism just doesn't function at its best, physically, mentally or spiritually.

It's like running a car without servicing it. It goes after a fashion but hardly at its best. To get the best results you consult the maker's handbook and do the servicing at the proper mileage.

So we need to consult our Maker's handbook and see what the Bible has to say about the marvellous mechanism called man.

The simile of the machine stops when we look at the Bible and see, as we have already in the first chapter, 'Let us make man in our image'. Man is in the likeness of God, and on the seventh day

God rested from all his work which he had done.

God finished the work of creation and rested. It wasn't the rest of idleness. If it had been the whole world would have fallen apart. God stopped creating and started sustaining.

In the same way if you stop your car and leave it for the period required for servicing but do nothing to it, it will probably go just the same – only worse! Rest is not idleness.

Using Sunday positively

Rest doesn't end with not working on Sunday. It involves how we use the day. Most keen Christians are probably far too busy on the Lord's day. If we are to be spiritually refreshed and physically and mentally rested we need to do different things from those we do all the week.

If your work is heavy manual type you probably need physical rest. On the other hand, if your occupation ties you to a lathe or bench all week then you will probably need some physical activity.

If you live in the centre of a large city you will need fresh air. Recognizing this need, the leaders of the Mayflower Settlement at Canning Town in the East End of London acquired an ancient motor coach and the congre-

Knocking-off time

gation would go together to nearby Epping Forest. Often they would have a communion service there in some forest clearing.

Obviously worship is the centre of Sunday. You need to rest in the Lord. This is a very positive commandment.

Remember the sabbath day to keep it holy.

When we worship it should not be alone. Jesus went to the synagogue on the sabbath, it states time and time again in the Gospels, and adds 'as was his custom'. Shop-floor Christians are no different from others in needing this fellowship, this sharing worship. The writer to the Hebrews says, 'Don't stop coming together.' And certainly time should be spent with your own family, enjoying each other's company.

All this should mean we return to work refreshed in body, mind and spirit.

We may be a little reluctant to leave the fellowship we have been enjoying. If we have met with our Lord in worship and Christian brothers and sisters in fellowship and spent time with our families, Monday morning should only be tinged with slight regret it is over. If you have a real 'Monday-morning feeling', have a careful look at your Sunday. It's probably too busy.

Sunday work

God knows best. Perhaps that is stating the obvious to Christians, but here are one or two bits of human wisdom to buttress the doubting.

At one of the most crucial periods in this country's history, namely on 29 May 1941 during World War II, the Minister of Labour, Mr Ernest Bevin, told the House of Commons that Sunday work in arms factories was to be cut down as much as possible and that, generally, a seven-day working week did not increase production.

Later the same year a select committee of the House of

Commons reported: 'No man can work seven days a week and maintain his output.'

I don't believe God gave impossible laws. However, modern society has made it impossible for everyone to take the same day off. Certain work has to be done. We all use electricity, gas and water on Sunday, eat meals cooked on Sunday and, of course, Jesus made the point that it was right to heal on the sabbath. So hospital staff, ambulance men and so on work.

But it isn't quite as simple as that. As a friend of mine who works for the Electricity Board says, 'The same electricity that lights the operating theatre drives the brewery pumps.' We just can't entirely separate the good from the bad, the necessary from the unnecessary. That should not stop us from trying.

It is obviously much better for everybody to maintain and extend the idea of one day when as much work as is humanly possible is shut down. Because with Joe on 'A' shift, Dad on 'B' shift and Mum doing part-time in 'Brown's Canteen', the family are not resting together.

It was much the same in Isaiah's day and God speaking through him said,

If you turn back your foot from the sabbath,
from doing your pleasure on my holy day,
and call the sabbath a delight
and the holy day of the Lord honourable;
if you honour it, not going your own ways
or seeking your own pleasure, or talking idly;
then you shall take delight in the Lord,
and I will make you ride upon the heights of the earth.

Christians will refrain from working on Sundays whenever possible, but we share a responsibility for those who do work and for the sin of society in this matter. We can't just opt out. It's put neatly by Isaiah:

And it shall be, as with the people, so with the priest;
as with the slave, so with his master;
as with the maid, so with her mistress;
as with the buyer, so with the seller;
as with the lender, so with the borrower;
as with the creditor, so with the debtor.

Or, as David Sheppard has put it, 'We are involved with the rest of the community because God has deliberately wrapped us together in the bundle of life.'

We can make certain that if we have to work on Sunday we have a rest day during the week, and also do all within our power to see that other people's work is kept to a minimum. Other people will, of course, include Mum and the rest of the family. The one thing we must not do is to judge those who work on Sunday, for often we share their sin (if sin it is), even if only by using what they produce.

I have on odd occasions worked on Saturday afternoon to get an urgent job out rather than work on Sunday, but by doing so I have made it possible for the next phase of production (inspection and test) to be carried out on Sunday. True, the inspectors could have declined to work, but by removing pressure from myself I made a way for pressure to be applied to them.

The need is to consider our own action carefully and not to condemn others, but rather to influence them to think through their own position. We can learn much of our responsibility for the sins of our communities from men like Moses, Job and Nehemiah (see the Bible passages listed at the end of this chapter).

Not just Sunday

The Rev. Eddie Stride said recently that 'only now have we begun to catch up on the holidays the Old Testament Jews enjoyed and which God had ordained'.

Some Christians have tended to regard leisure as sinful.

' "Six days you shall labour." Brother, if you do a five-day week you're plain idle!'

Take a good look at the facts in the Bible. The whole tenor of life was more leisurely. There were feast days, sabbath years of rest for the land, years of jubilee. The people enjoyed holy-days without dividing or making false divisions between the sacred and the secular. The Feast of Booths is a good example, when the people camped out for a week in leafy tents.

That visit of Jesus with His parents to Jerusalem was a casual, joyful, unhurried time of fellowship, meeting with the family and worship. You get something of the informality of the occasion when you realize they did not worry when Jesus never turned up to eat the first day of the return trip. I can imagine Joseph saying to Mary, 'Don't worry, dear, that boy won't go hungry. He'll find somebody who will feed Him.'

'*They went every year*', Luke says.

Then there was Solomon. He never found all that wisdom about beasts, and birds, reptiles and fish by keeping his nose to the grindstone six days a week, fifty-two weeks a year. You have to take time to observe nature.

What is this life if, full of care,
We have no time to stand and stare?

In many trades a sharper distinction between work and leisure came about when the place of work and the home (the place of leisure) were separated. In the days prior to the industrial revolution very often home was the place of work and leisure.

Many of the older houses in Bethnal Green, East London, still have long windows in the upper storeys where the weavers of the district set up their looms for maximum light. Recently when I was in Nottingham a local vicar pointed out to me similar types of cottages where the lacemakers used to live and work.

David, when he wrote, 'The Lord's my shepherd, I'll not want', was probably working (minding his sheep), worshipping God and following his leisure pursuit of composing, although I very much doubt whether any employer in this day and age would be overjoyed if you took to composing ballads or poetry whilst minding a machine in the factory. Times have changed and it would be neither safe nor sensible.

God hasn't changed and God cares and He still wants His people to have leisure.

It's a great temptation to work a lot of overtime. It helps especially if you are an apprentice or improver and the money is tight. Often strong pressure is put on by management to do excessive overtime, to take money instead of your full entitlement of holidays.

I believe, in the long run, neither you nor the firm gain by this. '*All work and extra pay makes Jack a dull boy!*'

A young Christian I knew in management put in quite long hours for the company but insisted in the end on having some leisure time. As he put it, 'It's all roundabouts and no swings.' His immediate boss complained, 'You don't put the firm first.' Of course he didn't. 'You shall worship God and him only.' In fact, the company lost a very devoted and intelligent servant because they had their priorities wrong. He left the firm.

In the same way, I know a man who is a branch secretary of his Trade Union, and generally claims to be in the forefront of the fight for better conditions for the workers. Yet he never misses a minute's overtime and is the laughing stock of the workshop because of the way he grovels for the foreman's favour when people are wanted in for Sunday.

It's the balance that's important.

Balancing Solomon's

> *a little sleep, a little slumber, a little folding of the hands to rest, and poverty will come upon you like a vagabond,*

with our Lord's order,

come away to a lonely place and rest a while.

Bible passages to look up

Sunday rest

Genesis 2:2–3
Exodus 20:8–11; 31:2–7; 34:21
Isaiah 58:13–14

Sunday work: wrong and right

Leviticus 26:34–43
Nehemiah 13:15–22
Matthew 12:1–13
John 7:14–24

Leisure

Leviticus 23:25:1–22
Mark 6:31

Responsibility for others

Genesis 18:22–33
Numbers 14:11–20
Nehemiah 1:5–11
Luke 23:34

Useful booklets

Industry and Sunday (Lord's Day Observance Society)
A New Look at Sunday (Crusade Reprint; Evangelical Alliance)

8 'Out of the wet'

I suppose Rudyard Kipling is a bit 'old hat' today but he's my favourite poet and I'm not willing to argue the toss about whether his verse is doggerel or not – it's just great. I've devoured *The Jungle Book* – not the Walt Disney version but the real McCoy, where the animals had real dignity. I was glad of 'Tommy' when in the RAF and feeling the civilian population unsympathetic. I love 'Puck's Song' . . . but I'm getting on a favourite hobby-horse. All I really want to say is, recently I came across a Kipling poem that really did things for me. At least, I came across a few lines of it in *Toward the Conversion of England* and a librarian traced the rest.

'Mulholland's Contract' is about a tough deck-hand on a cattle-boat.

For the lower deck is the dangerousest, requirin' constant care,
An' give to me as the strongest man, though used to drink and swear.

During a gale, the cattle pens broke and, the cattle crazed and milling about, Mulholland made a contract with God.

An' by the terms of the Contract, as I have read the same,
If He got me to port alive I would exalt His Name,
An' praise His Holy Majesty till further orders came.

Well, the cattle-drover deckhand miraculously survived the storm and the cattle's horns and hoofs. Then, after seven weeks in a Seamans' Hospital,

An' I spoke to God of our Contract, an' He says to my prayer:
'I never puts on My ministers no more than they can bear.
So back you go to the cattle-boats an' preach My Gospel there.'

So back he went to the place where he knew it would be hard, the place where he was known, and the place that needed the gospel desperately. He didn't go eagerly:

I didn't want to do it, for I knew what I should get;
An' I wanted to preach religion, handsome an' out of the wet;
But the Word of the Lord were laid on me, an' I done what I was set.

The bit that got me was, '*I wanted to preach religion, handsome an' out of the wet*'. I know just how he felt and I expect you do. It's not so bad in the church atmosphere, among Christian friends (although even then we are a bit slow to praise His holy majesty), but at work!

You shall be my witnesses in Jerusalem and in all Judea and Samaria.

If Jerusalem is our home and Judea our neighbourhood, work is Samaria, the mixed nation that vaguely acknowledges our God and despises us. Sometimes we have richly deserved their contempt as the Jews so often deserved the contempt of the Samaritans.

It's not an easy place at all to talk about Jesus Christ, about what He means to you and what He has done for you by dying on a cross. Paul wrote to the Corinthians,

It's folly to the Gentiles.

If I may return to the cattle-boat, it illustrates part of the answer.

The skippers say I'm crazy, but I can prove 'em wrong,
For I am in charge of the lower deck with all that doth belong –
Which they would not give to a lunatic, and the competition so strong!

In other words, Mulholland says, 'I do a first-class job of work. Look at me, doesn't my work show I'm sane, well balanced?' It's the mark of a Christian that he works well. Paul says,

You are an open letter about Christ.

Our friends at work don't read the Bible, they don't see Jesus, but they do see us. How we work. How we speak. How we act.

They will ask questions. 'John, why do you . . . ?' 'Pete, why don't you . . . ?' 'Ray, what makes you . . . ?'

David, a very bright young man, was promoted to production engineer of a company I worked for. The job was tough and exciting and the pace furious. He was travelling to another branch of the firm with the production manager when his boss said, 'I've been watching you for the past month, you never swear or lose your temper. Why?' David had the opportunity and took it to tell of the One who was in charge of his lips and his life.

In doing so he was obeying Peter's command,

Be ready at any time to give a quiet and reverent answer to any man who wants a reason for the hope that you have within you.

'Quiet and reverent', he says. Old Mulholland hadn't read that part of the Bible!

I have been smit an' bruised, as warned would be the case.
An' turned my cheek to the smiter exactly as Scripture says;

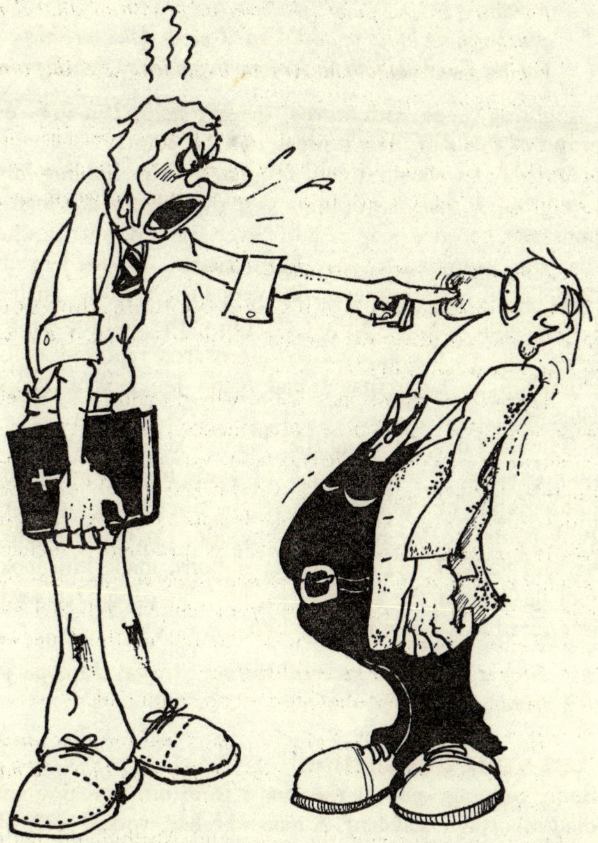

'Give a quiet and reverent answer . . .'

But, following that, I knocked him down an' led him up
to Grace.
An' we have preaching on Sundays whenever the sea is
calm,
An' I use no knife or pistol an' I never take no harm;
For the Lord abideth back of me to guide my fighting arm.

Fighting, even with words, doesn't help. I'm not very proud of this story but it illustrates the point.

One day I walked into our forge to find Joe holding forth to a group of lads his opinion that the Bible was a load of nonsense, because people hadn't even learned to write when that was supposed to have been written. I waded in and demolished his argument with very little trouble. In fact, I was going so well I didn't even hear the bell for dinner-time. One of the apprentices afterwards reported to the workshop at large that I had made Joe look a 'proper Charlie'.

The next day, knowing that Joe was keenly interested in photography, I took a book to work full of marvellous photographs of biblical discovery – things dug up in the Bible lands, etc. Joe swept it on one side. 'I'm not interested', he said flatly. I had cut him to ribbons, made him look a fool in front of the apprentices, hurt his pride. He wasn't interested and I don't blame him.

Give a quiet and reverent answer . . . for the hope you have.

'Let your light shine'

Some time ago one of the chaps from our machine shop died in a tragic accident. A man who had worked with him went to the memorial service and reported back: 'I always admired him, he was a good man, but I never knew all the work he did for old folk, and he was a sort of preacher too. All the people at this chapel were so happy; it was more like a wedding than a funeral.

'One old boy about eighty stood up and spoke; all he seemed sorry about was old Jim had beat him to it up there. My missis and I couldn't get over it. We laid in bed talking about it till two o'clock in the morning. If I ever joined a church that would be the sort I would go to.'

We checked around the various Christians in the plant, members of the Christian Fellowship, people who had known him for years. Not one had a clue that Jim was a lay preacher and a Christian.

'I always admired him . . . but I never knew.'

> *Let your light so shine before men that they may see your good works and give glory to your Father in heaven.*

I had gone to a house to repair a typewriter and while the lady of the house got the inevitable 'cuppa' I glanced round the room. A copy of *Pilgrim's Progress* and a Bible caught my attention. 'Are you a Christian?' I asked her when she brought the refreshment. She was and she couldn't get her story out quickly enough.

Her husband had got a new job as a warehouseman. The first evening he told her the chap he worked with was all right. Didn't talk much, though; just got on with his work. Bit queer, really. By the following week he had come home telling her this chap was religious and wanted him to go along to his church. He was impressed and had accepted the invitation.

'Well', she said, 'I wasn't keen. I didn't want him going all religious on me, so I went with him. Didn't want him doing anything silly!' That Sunday they both accepted Christ as their Saviour in the workmate's Pentecostal church.

> *A city set on a hill cannot be hid.*

Bible passages to look up

The commission

Matthew 28:16–20 Acts 1:8

The life

Matthew 5:13–16
2 Corinthians 3:3
Titus 2:3–8

The lip

Ezekiel 3:4–5, 16–21; 33:1–16
Romans 10:8–17
1 Peter 3:15

9 'I alone am left'

It is easy to feel like Elijah in a factory and think that everybody else has bowed the knee to the modern-day Baals. You are probably wrong, just as Elijah was wrong.

Vic Hammond of the Workers' Christian Fellowship tells of receiving two letters in one week from Christians asking to be registered as 'lone members' at the same firm. Naturally he was happy to inform them they were not alone.

A Christian Fellowship is the thing to join, or start, if you have the 'I alone am left' feeling.

I've sat with two others under an assembly line in a motor plant and met with forty or more in a small chapel near the works. The numbers are not the important thing; it's the unity that counts.

When I first joined my present firm I found the going tough. I had been away from the trade some time and was not finding it easy to get back into the swing of things. My fingers were all thumbs and I was as slow as a snail. Moreover I was on piece-work where speed means money.

I was sitting at a table in the canteen one dinner-hour when a man approached me and said, 'Were you wearing a different jacket yesterday?' Rather surprised, I agreed I had been. 'Did I see a Scripture Union badge in the lapel?' he asked. He had indeed! 'Why don't you come along to the

Christian Fellowship?' he asked. The short answer was that I did not know there was a Fellowship because I hadn't looked at the notice-board.

It is a source of constant amazement to me that notice-boards are so seldom read. I would read ours regularly if I could remember where it was!

Seriously, it is good to find others who share both your faith and work (that's not quite what James meant when he said 'Faith without works is dead!'). It is useful to meet together, talk, pray and share a concern for your fellow-workers. We can also share our work problems, for if we only talk 'religion' we are missing out on the wholeness of our faith.

I shared my problem and found another chap just out of the forces who was having the same bother. I've always found just seeing another person across the yard or over the other side of the workshop and to know he is 'one in Christ' is a real help.

Sometimes these meetings can become ingrown; it's a thing we must constantly watch.

It was a conference of Christian Fellowships and we had reached the discussion stage. 'At our place', said one lad very proudly, 'we have a very good programme. Monday lunch-time we meet for prayer; Tuesday is Bible study day. On Wednesday we usually have a speaker. Thursday another prayer meeting.' 'And when do you talk to the blokes you work with?' interrupted a voice.

The voice was right. We need balance; we must reach out to others. The salt needs sprinkling. Christians aren't supposed just to get pickled in a brine tub.

Perhaps sick-visiting can be organized if the firm doesn't already have a scheme, or members can be encouraged to take part if a scheme already exists.

Film shows are another activity that is sometimes profitable. We ran some in co-operation with the Photographic Section of the Sports and Social Club. In fact, their secretary brought in more outsiders than we did on one occasion.

A change in the style of meeting can help.

It was with some doubt that we decided to accept the suggestion of the secretary of the local church where we met in the dinner-hour. It was a matter that was discussed at some length. A year finally passed by before we made the momentous decision at our Annual General Meeting. Yes, one of their ladies could come and make us a cup of tea!

Eth's arrival was like a breath of fresh air. Our intention was that she should make tea in the hall kitchen and convey it to us in the vestry at the rear of the church where we sat neatly in rows facing the speaker. 'Tea will be stone cold', complained Eth, who was knocking on eighty years old and had the energy of a pocket battleship.

'Have the meeting in here', she ordered. We found ourselves seated around small tables in a room adjoining the kitchen, looking at each other instead of at the backs of each other's heads. Formality had fled; fellowship had arrived.

Come to think of it, that wasn't a breath of fresh air, that was a rushing mighty wind and God *was* in it.

The Fellowship must be open to all and be seen to be open to all, and all must be welcome.

One Fellowship refused the employers' offer of official company recognition because the management insisted on a separate meeting for office workers. The Fellowship was right. There is neither Jew nor Greek, factory nor office; we are all one in Christ Jesus.

Naturally different lunch-hours, shift work, size of plant, etc., may make it necessary for different groups to meet separately, but that is circumstance, not policy. Joint meetings should be held from time to time, perhaps in the evening or at weekends to demonstrate the fact of unity.

Snobbishness

Our Carol Service is always a rushed, cheerful affair and, having learned from Eth, we not only had tea but sausage rolls and mince pies on the tables for our lunch-time guests. Our opening carols were kept moving briskly by a song leader. Then the chairman rose: 'It's good to have with us two of our top management, for the first time I think (it wasn't!). We greatly appreciate their presence; we realize they are busy men, their time is precious . . .' and on and on it went.

The shadow of James hovered over the meeting.

> *Don't ever attempt, my brothers, to combine snobbery with faith in our glorious Lord Jesus Christ! . . . If you pay special attention to the well dressed man saying, 'Please sit here – it's an excellent seat', and say to the poor man, 'You stand over there, please, or if you must sit, sit on the floor . . . .'*

It is right, of course, to welcome *all our guests* at our meetings. It is right to give honour where it is due as the scripture reminds us, but not to exalt one above another. On the occasion I have just mentioned we had a number of outsiders in and I personally felt extremely uncomfortable about their lack of welcome.

The boot can be on the other foot. Another time a Fellowship member, a supervisor, came to me rather embarrassed. He didn't want to be standoffish, he wasn't standing on his dignity, but he did find it rather difficult when walking through the works with other management people to have a labourer shout across, 'Oi, dozy! Come 'ere a minute.'

We need to be very careful to give honour where it is due. If we are privileged to call our Christian brother Tom, Dick or Harry in the Fellowship, they are still Mr Hornby-Smythe, Greenwood or Butterworth on the factory floor and we are doubly careful not to expect any preferential treatment because we are 'one in Christ'.

I once asked a shop steward from Rubery Owen if being a Christian made any difference to promotion chances.

'Yes', he replied. 'It makes it more difficult. The boss is determined not to show any favouritism.'

Another important by-product of fellowship is that we find our particular branch of the vine is not so different from other branches and our grapes aren't all that sweeter. That which unites is so much greater than that which separates. It's a great game to guess which chap belongs to brand 'X' and which brand 'Y' and how often you can be wrong! In fact, you seldom remember there are any labels except 'Christian'.

We are not divided, all one body we.

Starting a Fellowship

I wrote at the beginning of this chapter, 'a Christian Fellowship is the thing to join, or start'; as with all Christian activity, I believe it starts with prayer. Not as an excuse for inactivity but to seek guidance for activity.

You will need at least one other Christian in the firm before you can meet together, to state the obvious. That does not mean you cannot do anything. You can prepare, and the Workers Christian Fellowship has gained a great deal of expertise in this field. They will willingly advise you and you can enrol as a lone member; the address is at the end of the chapter.

'And we forbade him'

From time to time I have found myself defending Christian Fellowships from attack by supporters of the Industrial Chaplaincy point of view. On other occasions I have strongly championed Industrial Chaplains when criticism came from Christian Fellowship enthusiasts. Each side has its own gory tale to tell of the devastation left by the other.

A lay pastor who worked in the motor industry was talking with me one day and I mentioned the possibility of local clergy obtaining permission to visit the factory regularly. He immediately retorted, 'We don't want the dog collars in the works.' I gathered that 'dog collars' were only slightly less obnoxious than stink bombs from the way he wrinkled his nose.

I have written at some length about Christian Fellowship because I belong to one and I am enthusiastic. However, there are other Christian organizations working in industry and doing valiant work. The Industrial Chaplains I have already mentioned. The London City Mission has missioners working in various industries and I expect other City Missions have also. There is Outreach to Industry, SLIM and various others. Not to be forgotten is the local vicar, minister or pastor who visits his local factory. His line of country may be personal evangelism, getting alongside or just trying to understand the working life of the people he ministers to.

We need every possible avenue of Christian activity and they need our support.

> '. . . *And we forbade him because he was not following us.' But Jesus said, 'Do not forbid him . . . . For he that is not against us is for us.'*

Bible passages to look up

Fellowship and loneliness

1 Kings 19:10, 14, 18

Acts 18:1–4; 28:14–15

Tasty Christianity

Matthew 5:13

Mark 9:49–50

John 17:15–24

Vision in the work

John 4:35; 21:3–6

1 Corinthians 9:19–23

Impartiality

Romans 10:11–12

Galatians 2

James 2:1–9

Different ministries

Mark 9:38–41

John 21:20–23

Further information

Workers Christian Fellowship
113 Whitchurch Gardens
Edgware
Middlesex HA8 6PG

10 Trade Unions

Who is the worst-paid man today?
With haggard look and hair turned grey,
Who's blamed when things do not go right?
Who gets no rest by day or night?
Though never having been to college
He must possess the widest knowledge
On rates of pay and hours of labour
And how to keep peace with one's neighbour,
Of Income Tax and how to pay it,
What's best to say, and when to say it,
The how and which and why and when
Of all the problems known to men.
If with the foreman he's agreed,
He's sold the men or been weak-kneed.
When for the men he tries to cater,
He's called a blinking agitator.
Who is the chap? What! Don't you know him?
Or how much you really owe him?
This chap, whose torment is assured,
Is no-one else than your shop steward! ANON.

Well, that's one view – not the one usually gathered from newspapers or the television. What about the Unions? Where does the Christian take his stand?

First I had better come clean! I'm a shop steward so I'm a committed pro-Union man.

Conditions of employment existed 200 years ago which lead to bloody revolution in other European countries but, thank God, we were spared them. Gradually the Trade Union movement fought and obtained negotiating rights for workers. It was a long and bitter struggle and some of the bitterness still persists. This is no place to go into details but a list of useful books will be found at the end of the chapter if you want to know more – and I hope you will!

Trade Unions were born or evolved along with the Industrial Revolution to protect workers from exploitation, both in hours of work and wages.

Christians have been both for and against Unions from the start.

So you had Joseph Arch, a Primitive Methodist lay preacher, founding the Warwickshire Agriculture Labourers' Union and being strongly supported by Roman Catholic Cardinal Manning and Canon Girdlestone of the Church of England. They were strongly opposed by the Bishop of Gloucester (Dr Elliot) and most of the country parsons.

The Tolpuddle Martyrs were Methodist lay preachers (they were transported to Australia for trying to form a Trade Union branch).

The greatest factory reformer of them all, Lord Shaftesbury, was against the Trade Unions as was William Wilberforce who led the campaign to outlaw slavery.

So it has continued to this day, some for – some against.

God cares

What is clear is that God is deeply concerned about justice in work and wages.

The people of Israel were told not to keep back the wages of the hired servant until the morning, presumably so that he could buy what he needed for supper and be up in the market-place bright and early next day for another job.

When Moses restated the law before the people entered the promised land, he said,

> *You shall not oppress a hired servant who is poor and needy, whether he is one of your brethren or one of the sojourners.*

The testimony continues throughout the Bible law and prophet, Old and New Testament. God cares about people; James says in chapter 5, verse 4, of his letter:

> *Behold, the wages of the labourers who mowed your fields, which you kept back by fraud, cry out; and the cries of the harvesters have reached the ears of the Lord of hosts.*

'Let all things be done decently and in order'

Just as in modern society we have found it necessary to set up police forces and law courts to assure that the commandments not to steal, cheat and kill are observed, so I believe Trade Unions and Employer Federations make possible orderly employer and employee relationship.

With our vast industrial concerns it just is not possible for each man to negotiate wages, hours of work, holidays, etc., directly with his employer. Neither would it be practical to do it individually with supervisors.

I recall one manager telling his shop stewards that he wasn't prepared to talk to them. He would talk money to the men individually. For a couple of days a continual stream of men went to his office to ask for rises. He gave up!

Obviously one spokesman is a better way. In any case, what about the chap who knows his job but is quite unable to speak up for himself? In the matter of fixing holiday rotas, safety aspects, workshop cleanliness and a thousand and one other things, it cannot and must not be 'every man for himself'.

We could leave it to the employer to be just to his workers, but the employer is a sinner as much as the employed. The pressures of competition force him to keep his costs as low as possible and one of his costs is labour. If he knows his competitors must also pay Union rates he is at no disadvantage.

In point of fact, employers have their own Federation which negotiate with Unions at national level. Some mammoth companies like the motor and chemical ones deal directly with Union headquarters as well.

Some would quote Paul, 'Be ye not unequally yoked together with unbelievers', but does it apply to all our associations? If so, the doctor must leave the British Medical Association and the solicitors the Law Society. Taken to its logical conclusion we should leave every institution, as indeed the Exclusive Brethren have.

The Revised Standard Version renders it 'Do not be mismated with unbelievers' which, to me, rings quite a different bell . . . wedding bells!

'Everybody out'

'A Christian must not strike. The Bible forbids it; it's in Timothy.' The speaker was earnest and sure of his facts, and a quick look at 1 Timothy 3:3 confirmed them.

> *. . . not given to wine, no striker, not greedy of filthy lucre.*

Well, his reference was right so I went a step further. Next test, context. What does the verse before say?

> *A bishop then must be blameless . . . .*

So it's about bishops. Imagine the Archbishop of Canterbury on the picket line: 'PARITY WITH ROME', 'EQUAL PAY FOR THE MASSES'. Even my vivid imagination could not swallow that. There must be another answer. Third test, compare versions. We have looked at the Authorized; what does the RSV say?

No drunkard, not violent, but gentle.

'Not violent' = 'no striker'. Saved again! This passage isn't about industrial relations but the qualification of church leaders, and they must not be boozers or punch-up specialists.

The question remains: What is the Christian attitude to strikes and, of course, lockouts?

By definition a strike is when workmen withhold their labour collectively. A lockout is when an employer withholds work from his employees. In both cases to gain some advantage from the other party.

I have already mentioned that Trade Unions make possible negotiation for justice in the matter of wages, conditions of employment, hours of work, etc. To do this they must be able to apply some sanctions.

The only possible bargaining power the ordinary worker has is the withdrawal of his work or the threat to do so. He has no other weapon. Like all weapons it should be used only when all else fails.

So highly is this prized in our democratic society that the right to strike is written into our law. Likewise, when a company feels its employees are going beyond reasonable action, it must have the right to say, Enough! We withhold your work.

So recently, after a series of Union meetings during working hours had limited the production of daily newspapers, the employers shut down all the national newspaper presses until the men agreed to work normally.

War

A strike is war; negotiations have stopped. There are no neutrals among those involved. If you go in to work you are on the firm's side; if you stay out you are with the men.

'Thou shalt not strike . . .?'

Tempers get frayed, demands on both sides become more extreme, positions which have been fluid become hardened.

The Christian must not go home and lie low until it's all over. Never was salt more necessary, never did light need shedding more. He ought to attend every meeting, speak whenever he feels he usefully can, to groups or individuals, or at a mass meeting.

The agonizing choice of 'who is my neighbour?' does not have to be made. The boss and your workmate are both your neighbour.

You may well be a better neighbour to your boss by forcing him to concede to a just demand than by giving in. Equally you may need to be a good neighbour to your fellow-workers by opposing an excessive pay-rise that will damage the enterprise you work for, the economy of the country and those who have not the power to demand increases.

It seems to me that the man who goes into work during a strike is an embarrassment to the employer and has broken faith with his Union.

Tom Hamm, a member of the executive of the Stevedores' Union, was involved in the negotiations which led to a completely new pay structure for London dock-workers. Hot on the news of the signing of the agreement the dockers struck. Tom hurried to the dock gates to persuade his colleagues to return to work but without success. He was telling a group of us fellow-Christians about this later when someone asked, 'Did you go in?' 'No', Tom replied. 'I could have done but I stood by the lads.'

Obviously there is much more one could say about strikes but apprentices are not usually involved because they are indentured. So I will close with a couple of warnings.

Regard reports in newspapers about strikes with the same reserve you use when they report religious meetings. One strike makes news; the thousand and one peaceful settlements do not.

Voice of the people

Certainly if the wrong people control Trade Unions wrong decisions will be taken and wrong action follow.

All Trade Union officers are elected by the membership, but only by that part of the membership that bothers to vote. In fact, this is just a tiny minority. Consider: there is not one Communist Member of Parliament yet a lot of Communists in Trade Union leadership. Why? Because Trade Union leaders are usually elected by 0·5% or less of the membership, while the General Election turn-out is between 60% and 80%.

There are more Christians in industry than Communists yet hardly any (*hardly* any, God has His servants) are in key Union positions.

I believe it was Burke who said,

> *All that is needed for evil to succeed is for good men to do nothing.*

To return to the shop steward. He is the elected representative on the shop floor. Although that poem is somewhat exaggerated he is there to protect the interests of the men, to obtain justice for them on all sorts of issues including safety, wage rates and working conditions. Until recently nobody had ever spelt out the limits of the shop steward's job. It varies from one Union to another and between different factories.

Recently the Commission on Industrial Relations has been looking at shop stewards and have published a report called – surprise! surprise! – *Shop Stewards*. The thing that comes out loud and clear is that he is the link between management and shop floor on grievances, both individual and group, and on communicating management thinking to his members. This means he meets management men (foremen and supervisors) fairly regularly.

So it's essential to have a man who won't blow his top

at the least provocation, who isn't self-seeking, doesn't harbour grudges; who is genuinely seeking the just settlement and not merely provoking trouble; who is neither scared of the men nor the boss. A lover of his neighbour – the *management* neighbour and the *worker* neighbour – which seems to me a made-to-measure job for a Christian. And, in fact, some are shop stewards.

Don't just be a card-carrying member. Your representative will need your moral support and prayer. Perhaps some day God will call you to serve Him and your fellow-workers in this way, so learn what you can about it.

For too long many Christians have sat on the touch-line and booed, but the game is played on the pitch. That's where the mud is, that's where the bruises and cuts are collected. It is, however, the only place to be if you want to win the game.

Bible passages to look up

Wages and oppression

Leviticus 19:13–15
Deuteronomy 24:14–15
Proverbs 22:20–25
Malachi 3:5
James 5:1–5

Love

1 Corinthians 13:4–7

Unequal yoking

Ezekiel 34 (read the whole chapter; remember that the shepherds are princes, the sheep are the people)
2 Corinthians 6:14

Some books of interest

David Winter, *The Cross and the Sickle* (Falcon Booklets)

The History of TUC. A Pictorial Survey (Trade Union Congress)

G. M. Trevelyan, *English Social History* (Longmans)

Arthur Bryant, *English Saga* (Collins)
Commission on Industrial Relations, *Shop Stewards Report* (HM Stationery Office)
H. F. R. Catherwood, *The Christian in Industrial Society* (Tyndale Press)

11 'Not a sparrow falls'

'One thousand people die.' 'One million injured.' No! it isn't a tidal wave or a cyclone disaster. It is just the annual accident rate in British industry. And accidents are avoidable.

It's not a case of binding up, pouring in oil and bringing him to the inn. That indeed is done and very effectively in most factories, mines and building sites, but it is a little late. Rather, we need to stop the robbers who do the damage. Their names are Apathy, Greed, Familiarity, Ignorance and Pride. Get rid of those five and the casualty figure will plunge down.

What has it got to do with Christianity? It's that law again! The royal law 'You shall love your neighbour as yourself.' It's the self bit I would like to deal with first.

That manly (or womanly) body happens to be God's (you are bought with a price). It's His temple, not to be mutilated. Just as the Israelites were forbidden to mutilate their bodies for false gods, so yours must be kept whole. In any case, I guess you like having both hands, feet and eyes. So did the 11,000 who lost eyes last year, 45,000 who lost feet and 80,000 who lost hands.

She promised her husband she would never take off

Apathy, Greed, Familiarity, Ignorance, Pride

her wedding ring; in any case it was bad luck. She didn't take it off – a bench drill did. Hard luck? No, stupidity.

He could earn much more, work much faster if he removed the guard from the machine. He removed his arm at the elbow and can't earn at all now.

Most accidents are not as serious as those, some are more serious, even fatal, and they happen because people do not think it could happen to them.

Apathy

Let's look at apathy first. Both worker and management suffer from this. The worker who doesn't bother to wear goggles when doing jobs where a spark or a piece of metal, stone, brick, etc., is likely to fly. The management who fail to provide warning notices, goggles, visors or other protection. 11,000 eyes in one year.

I have been delighted beyond words in recent months to see great tough men on building sites wearing eye protectors and helmets. Road builders with day-glow jerkins on and toe-tector boots (they are boots with metal toecaps) to protect the feet from falling objects.

I recall an occasion at Fords where a man bought a pair of toe-tector shoes but kept them for best because they were new. On the line he wore a pair of sandals. Need I say more?

Apathy is leaving undone the thing you know ought to be done. As Christians we ought to always go the second mile to see that somebody is safe. You can't be overcareful.

When I approach one particular supervisor and say, 'I want a word with you', I see his face drop and if he can find a quick excuse he's away like a shot. If he can get away with a promise 'to do something about it', he will and nothing will be done. Yet when you finally nail him and follow him to the office, he picks up the phone and with a two-minute call, safety men, maintenance or whoever is needed to do the job are obtained. Jesus said we wouldn't be popular, and this is a realm where sometimes you have to be very unpopular.

Familiarity

We do tend to get used to things quickly. I'll always remember the first time I entered a huge car works. A clerk took me into the factory, under an assembly line, across a gangway (it looked more like the M1 than a gangway to me), round several more rows of roaring machines and said, 'Wait there till I come back.' He needn't have worried, I just stood rooted to the spot until he rescued me! I was amazed, overwhelmed, petrified.

Yet within a week I was an old hand. The hugeness had receded and I could find my way about with ease.

That's the danger-point when we lose that sense of awe. Never get over-familiar with electricity, machinery or your governor. Keep a healthy respect for each and think before you act.

Bert had served his time in the Navy, battleships, subs, the lot. Been down the mines and run industry; he was knocking on for retirement age. 'Is the current all off?' I ask. 'Of course, do yer think I'm daft?' I ducked my head into the electronics compartment, reached up my screwdriver . . . BANG! I shot out like a banshee in full flight and about the same colour!

I developed a system after that. First check the mains were off myself, then pull out all possible plugs in case somebody switched on. A third precaution was to make sure Bert, or whoever it was, was a safe distance away, preferably in the canteen, or, if that could not be managed, engaged in telling his favourite tale of how he once got a shock of 600 volts, or was it 6,000 volts? I know it got more and more each time it was told!

Greed

Cutting corners, speeding up the job, making more piecework, getting overtired through too much overtime or taking an evening job to pay for the 'banger'.

'The love of money is the root of all evil' Paul said, and it's often the root of accidents.

Equally, the company that skimps on cleaning greasy floors, gangway marking, maintenance of machinery, guards, warning notices, is guilty before God.

A Christian friend of mine returned from India where he had been involved in building a power station. He was middle-aged and had great difficulty in finding a job. Eventually he obtained employment as a safety officer on a building site. One day he observed some planks were not properly secured on a scaffolding. He reported it, but nothing was done. He reported it again, but still it wasn't fixed. The next day a man trod on the end of the plank, it tipped and he fell and was injured. At the inquiry my friend duly told what had happened. 'We had it secured before the accident', said the boss. 'No, sir', my friend replied. That cost him his job but not his integrity. It cost the firm a lot of money in compensation which greed would have denied the injured man.

'Where ignorance is bliss, tis folly to be wise.' So runs the saying but, to go from sayings to songs, 'It ain't necessarily so', and it most definitely isn't in safety.

Unfortunately, out of 21,688 factories covered by Home Office Factory Inspectors, 15,826 have no safety service of any kind. This obviously is a very unsatisfactory state of affairs and one that Christians ought to work towards remedying.

In the meantime, as an individual you need to be informed. More than half the injuries in factories are to people handling goods. Anything from sprains and strains to slipped discs and hernias, nearly all could be avoided by correct lifting.

A spokesman for the Engineering Employers Federation said, 'It would save well over a million working days a year if everyone remembered to squat next time they picked up anything. The secret is to let leg and thigh muscles take the strain, not arms and back.' Add to that all the other injuries through ignorance and you will see it isn't bliss and wisdom excels folly, and wisdom comes from the Lord.

Pride

Rather – false pride! Like the refusal to wear a cap over long hair or to use an extractor when using dangerous materials. It's not 'cissy' to be safe. It's better to be laughed at than lose your eyes. Have you ever thought that pride lost Samson his sight, his freedom, his life?

It's vital not to laugh at people taking precautions. It's vital to take them yourself.

Over 20,000,000 days are lost in British industry through accidents. Geoffrey Goodman, writing in the *Daily Mirror*, highlighted the problem when he said, 'It is now odds on every worker having at least two significant accidents in his or her working life.'

Industrial diseases

'Eat a peck before you die' is an old saying about dirt. Whatever the truth of the matter regarding ordinary dirt, it is most certainly false regarding 'industrial dirt'.

Skin disease, chest complaints and so on are more and more being caused by chemicals and plastics as well as by the traditional industrial materials, cutting oils, etc.

A woman died of asbestosis. At the inquest it was discovered that she had never worked in the industry but her husband brought his overalls home to be washed, instead of allowing the firm to clean them with their special processes.

Cyril was noted throughout the firm for getting epoxy-resins everywhere when he mixed them. His fingers would run through his hair transferring it to his scalp. He was a bit of a joke. His body and hands are now covered with dermatitis, the skin red, cracked and flaky. It's no joke.

The answer is care and cleanliness. Always use barrier creams provided, wash frequently especially before and after going to the toilet, then use the barrier cream again. It's not cissy – it's sense.

Cleanliness is not merely next to godliness; it is a part of godliness.

Use respirators, masks, extractors and all other forms of provided protection. Inform your supervisor or safety officer if the protection isn't available.

Accidents are sudden, the result swift as a rule. Industrial diseases may take years to show themselves.

Some time ago, having read about the death of the woman from asbestosis, I became concerned about a job I did very occasionally which involved packing around an air heater with asbestos powder. My inquiries were not taken very seriously at first: 'We've been doing them for years; of course it's OK.' Eventually after much argument and pressure we contacted and had a visit by a factory inspector. He took one look, stepped smartly back out of harm's way and decreed extractors and respirators before any more was done.

A further time elapsed. The job became urgent and pressure was put upon me to do 'just one'. Fortunately the problem was solved by the Union Convenor discovering that the type of extractor we needed existed in another part of the factory and arrangements were made for me to do the job there. That was some time ago, and we now have a bay with excellent extractors and we have suitable respirators.

Today I saw one of the older men repairing a heater on his bench. I pointed out the dangers and that safety facilities were installed. 'That's all right, I'm being careful'.

he replied. As careful as the woman who washed her husband's overalls.

One is reminded of God's cry to the Israelites 'Why will you die?'

Before God you are responsible for yourself and your brother. If you have the opportunity to do a course on safety, take it. If you can serve on a Safety Committee at work consider whether this might be the Lord's will for you. In any case, think safety, act safety. You are your brothers' and sisters' keeper.

To fail to be safety-conscious or to ignore safety precautions is as much a sin as blasphemy or adultery, for James says,

> *Whoever knows what is right to do and fails to do it, for him it is sin.*

Bible passages to look up

Care of yourself
1 Corinthians 3:16–17; 6

Care for others
Exodus 21:27–36
Matthew 12:11–12

12 The one-man band

I am always highly amused by the old stunt of the actor playing all the parts in a play and changing his hat, cloak, beard, etc., as he takes the various roles. The big laugh always comes when he gets the wrong hat for the wrong character. Corny perhaps, but it reminds me rather of the temptation we all have to play all the parts.

Obviously this is something that will come to you later rather than immediately. God has his purpose for you; we have differing gifts and to do a few things well is better than doing the lot badly.

Moses had to discover this, and his father-in-law was the man who pointed out he couldn't do it all himself.

> *What you are doing is not good. You and the people with you will wear yourselves out, for the thing is too heavy for you; you are not able to perform it alone.*

Don't try to wear the leader of the Christian Fellowship hat, shop steward hat and vice-chairman of the Football Section jersey all at once. My wife thinks it very funny that I should offer such advice and when I declare (with some heat) that I've learned my lesson and I'm on a strict diet of jobs, she smiles and observes that she hasn't noticed any weight coming off me. Paul wrote:

Let us lay aside every weight, and sin which clings so closely, and let us run with perseverance the race that is set before us.

It certainly is easy to take on too much and it is equally easy to do nothing and leave it all to the other people. The important thing is that all we do should further God's kingdom and not hinder it.

The tail of the lion

We have covered quite a lot of ground in this book. We have seen that God is concerned about industry and the men and women in it. That we can't leave God at the factory gate; He is already inside anyway but you must not leave Christ outside. Perhaps you find the whole thing a bit daunting. You couldn't possibly cope, better to just keep yourself to yourself!

You will know about that cute little lizard, the chameleon. Nature has endowed him with a wonderful protection against his enemies. He just changes colour. As he gets onto a rock he goes brown, then across a patch of grass and his colour merges with the green background. The idea is attractive. Let's be a chameleon; nobody will notice. Peter tried it round a fire once when the night was chilly. It didn't work. The Lord turned and looked at Peter.

He was a middle management man, big and blustery, with a loud voice and plenty to say. That morning he had a different suit on and I spotted a small silver cross in the lapel and recognized it as one which was issued to celebrate our diocese jubilee.

'What church do you belong to?' I asked. He stopped in his tracks, looked furtively over his shoulder and whispered the name of a church some miles away. Not only was he a member, he was a churchwarden – a top man. His chameleon skin had slipped. That little silver badge had given him away.

We all will fail from time to time but that is no excuse for not trying. It is easy to fall, but His grace is sufficient for all our need, as Peter found after he had denied his Lord.

Industry is big, vast, complicated and altogether more exacting than school. Baden-Powell wrote in one of his books, 'Better the tail of the lion than the head of the mouse.' I believe he was referring to the progress of a Cub to the Scout troop. But when the lion is swishing its tail it can be rather uncomfortable if you are just the tuft at the end.

It is tough starting out in the working world but it's made no easier by hiding our colours. It won't be easy.

It wasn't easy for Jesus but consider again His words to the disciples in John's Gospel, chapters 15 and 16. After telling them that the world would hate them, persecute them, they would be scattered, have tribulation, He made this astounding statement:

Be of good cheer, I have overcome the world.

We are on the victory side.

Fierce may be the conflict,
Strong may be the foe.
But the King's own army
None can overthrow.